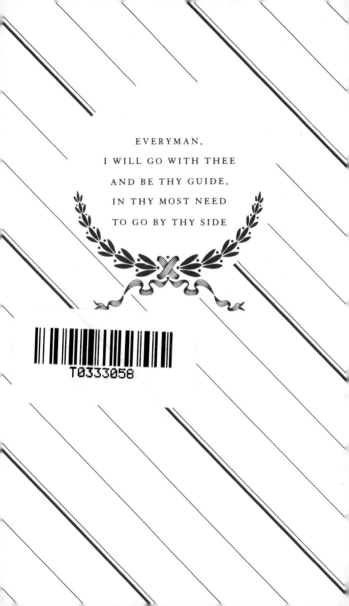

EVERYMAN,
I WILL GO WITH THEE
AND BE THY GUIDE,
IN THY MOST NEED
TO GO BY THY SIDE

T0333058

EVERYMAN'S LIBRARY
POCKET POETS

RAILWAY RHYMES

∙∙∙∙∙∙∙∙∙∙∙∙∙∙∙∙∙∙∙∙

EDITED BY PETER ASHLEY

EVERYMAN'S LIBRARY
POCKET POETS

This selection by Peter Ashley first published in Everyman's Library, 2007
© Everyman's Library, 2007

A list of acknowledgments to copyright owners appears at the back
of this volume.

ISBN 978-1-84159-778-2

A CIP catalogue record for this book is available from the British Library

Published by Everyman's Library,
50 Albemarle Street, London W1S 4BD

Distributed by Penguin Random House UK,
20 Vauxhall Bridge Road, London SW1V 2SA

Typography by Peter B. Willberg

Typeset by AccComputing, North Barrow, Somerset

Printed and bound in Germany by GGP Media GmbH, Pössneck

CONTENTS

8

NAVIGATING

OPENING HYMN

If you will listen to my song
I'll not detain you long.
On the 1st of May the folks did throng
To view the Oxford Railway.
And to have a ride – what a treat,
Father, mother, son and daughter
Along the line like one o'clock,
By fire, steam and water.

CHORUS:
Rifum, Tifum, mirth and fun,
Don't you wonder how it's done,
Carriages without horses run
On the Hampton and Oxford Railway.

From villages, and from the towns,
The gents and ladies flocked around.
And music through the air did sound,
Along the Oxford Railway.
There was bakers, butchers, nailers too,
Lots of gentlemen in blue,
And all did strive to get a view
Along the Oxford Railway.

An old woman peeping at the line
Said I wouldn't care a farthing,
But they destroyed my cottage fine
And cut away my garden,
Where I so many years did dwell
Growing lots of cabbages and potatoes,
But worse than all my daughter Nell
Went off with the navigators.

In Alcestor lives a bonny lass,
I think they call her Nancy,
Says she a trip upon the line
Greatly would please my fancy.
I will ride by steam and work by steam,
By steam I'll on be hurried,
And when I can a husband find
By steam I will be married.

And when the line is finished at both ends,
You may send your cocks and hens
And go and visit all your friends,
Your ducks and turkeys, pigs and geese,
To any part wherever you please –
You may also send your butter and eggs,
And they can ride who've got no legs
By the Hampton and Oxford Railway.

ON THE PROJECTED KENDAL AND
WINDERMERE RAILWAY

Is then no nook of English ground secure
From rash assault? Schemes of retirement sown
In youth, and 'mid the busy world kept pure
As when their earliest flowers of hope were blown,
Must perish; – how can they this blight endure?
And must he too the ruthless change bemoan
Who scorns a false utilitarian lure
'Mid his paternal fields at random thrown?
Baffle the threat, bright Scene, from Orrest-head
Given to the pausing traveller's rapturous glance:
Plead for thy peace, thou beautiful romance
Of nature; and, if human hearts be dead,
Speak, passing winds; ye torrents, with your strong
And constant voice, protest against the wrong.

THE SPECULATORS

The night was stormy and dark,
   The town was shut up in sleep:
Only those were abroad who were out on a lark,
   Or those who'd no beds to keep.

I pass'd through the lonely street,
   The wind did sing and blow;
I could hear the policeman's feet
   Clapping to and fro.

There stood a potato-man
   In the midst of all the wet;
He stood with his 'tato-can.
   In the lonely Haymarket.

Two gents of dismal mien,
   And dank and greasy rags,
Came out of a shop for gin,
   Swaggering over the flags:

Swaggering over the stones,
   These shabby bucks did walk;
And I went and followed those seedy ones,
   And listened to their talk.

Was I sober or awake?
    Could I believe my ears?
Those dismal beggars spake
    Of nothing but railroad shares...

Their talk did me perplex,
    All night I tumbled and tost,
And thought of railroad specs,
    And how money was won and lost.

'Bless railroads everywhere,'
        I said, 'and the world's advance;
    Bless every railroad share
        In Italy, Ireland, France;
For never a beggar need now despair,
    And every rogue has a chance.'

A JUST DISDAIN

Proud were ye, Mountains, when in times of old,
Your patriot sons, to stem invasive war,
Intrenched your brows; ye gloried in each scar:
Now, for your shame, a Power, the Thirst of Gold,
That rules o'er Britain like a baneful star,
Wills that your peace, your beauty, shall be sold,
And clear way made for her triumphal car
Through the beloved retreats your arms enfold!
Heard YE that Whistle? As her long-linked Train
Swept onwards, did the vision cross your view?
Yes, ye were startled; – and, in balance true,
Weighing the mischief with the promised gain,
Mountains, and Vales, and Floods, I call on you
To share the passion of a just disdain.

SONGS OF SOCIAL CHANGE

THE RAILWAY WHISTLE OR THE BLESSINGS OF HOT-WATER TRAVELLING

Of all the wonders of the age, there's nothing now so
    much the rage;
Both rich and poor seem all engaged about the
    Eastern Railway.
There's hissing here and whizzing there, and boiling
    water everywhere;
'Midst fire and smoke you crack your joke and what
    may happen no one cares,
For some blow down and some blow up, into a
    carriage haste and pop;
At the sound of the whistle off you start on the
    Eastern Counties Railway.

There's trains full half a mile in length, drawn by a
    fiery monster's strength;
Good luck to your soul, keep clear of the banks, for
    fear that you go over.
But if by chance such a thing occurs and you should
    roll among the furze,
How pleasant to be capsized thus, with pigs and
    passengers in one mess.

And while you're down in the valley below, how
  pleasant to hear the engine blow,
You mount up again and off you go on the Eastern
  Counties Railway.

But some poor simple souls may say 'tis a dangerous
  thing to travel this way;
If the rail give way or the boilers burst, there's
  nothing on earth can save us.
The money we paid from our poor pockets may send
  us in the air like rockets,
Our heads as empty as water buckets, our precious
  eyes knocked out the sockets.
But sure such people can have no sense, 'twill all be
  the same a hundred years hence,
What odds will it make, we can die but once; might as
  well be smashed by the Railway.

Farewell ye coaches, vans and waggons, farewell ye
  keepers of roadside inns,
You'll have plenty of time to repent your sins in
  charging poor travellers double.
Farewell ye blustering coachmen and guards that
  never knew how to use civil words,
You'll no more use your horns, you know, except to
  place upon your brows;

Take your lumbering vehicles off the road, neither you
    nor they were ever much good,
For how could you carry such fine, big loads, as to the
    wonderful Railways.

Let's not forget railway directors, and from all harm
    they will protect us,
They'll study never to neglect us, so dearly they love
    locomotion.
It's for our good they take such pains, and never do
    they think of gains,
And, if a few hundred should be slain, our wives and
    children they'll maintain.
Then happy and thankful may we be, such blessed
    invention we've lived to see;
To all other travel bid for ever goodbye, but the
    wonderful Eastern Railways.

ANON.

THE COCKNEY'S TRIP TO BRUMMAGEM

You Birmingham lads, come and listen awhile,
And I'll tell you a story will cause you to smile,
For the railroad they're going to open next spring
Will life up from London to Birmingham bring.

And sing fal the diddle lero, sing fal the diddle lay.

When the swell mob comes down, we must look out
  for squalls,
Or they'll bolt with the organ from out the Town Hall;
They think themselves clever in every feat,
But we'll show 'em one more, boys, we'll show 'em
  Moor Street.

So reckon on sport when the Cockneys come down,
For they're all very flash from the fop to the clown;
Whether tinkers or tailors or omnibus cads,
We can learn them a tune called *The Warwickshire lads*.

The Cockneys for boxing have long held the sway;
This railroad will help us to meet them half-way.
This much I can say without telling a crammer:
If they'll find the anvil, we'll find our own hammer.

They say every cock can crow on his own hill,
But they must not come here empty pockets to fill.
They may walk round our streets without trouble
    or pain;
They'll have something to do to walk round
    Hammer Lane.

We all know that London's a place of renown,
And for my own part, I will not run her down;
But I can't help thinking it'll be a queer thing
To be fighting with Cockneys in our old Bull Ring.

So now to conclude and finish my song,
May the railroad be finished before very long;
May London and Brummagem unite and join hands
And grow like the oak tree of our native land.

ANON.

THE WONDERFUL EFFECTS OF THE
LEICESTER RAIL ROAD

Of all the great wonders that ever were known –
And some wonderful things have occurred in this town –
The Leicester rail road it will beat them all hollow;
And the man who first thought on 't he was a fine fellow.

No drunken stage-coachmen to break people's necks,
Turned o'er into ditches, sprawled out on your backs;
No blustering guard that, through some mistake,
His blunderbuss fires if a mouse should but squeak.

No, no, my good friends, now this rail road is finished,
All coachmen and cattle henceforth shall be banished.
You may ride up to London in three hours and a quarter,
With nothing to drive but a kettle of water.

What a beautiful sight it is for to see
A long string of carriages on the railway,
All loaded with passengers, inside and out,
And moved by what comes from a tea-kettle's spout.

And then, what a lot of employment 'twill make,
The Leicester bricklayers may now undertake
To send ready-built houses to London by steam;
No doubt it will turn out a very good scheme.

Now any old woman that has enough sense
By raking and scraping to save eighteenpence,
In service in London if she has a daughter,
She may ride up and see her by this boiler of water.

The ostlers and innkeepers and such riff raff,
The rail road will blow them away, just like chaff;
They may 'list for Her Highness, the great Queen
    of Spain,
And curse the inventors of rail roads and steam.

Coach horses that eat up more corn in a year
Than would maintain three parts of the labouring poor,
They are all to go to the fellmonger's yard,
Where they will be rendered into good hog's lard.

And all coach proprietors who've rolled in wealth
Must ride upon donkeys for the good of their health,
And to keep up their spirits must strike up this theme
And curse all the railroads and boiling hot steam.

ANON.

THE NAVIGATORS

All you that delight in the railway making,
Come listen awhile to what I do sing;
In summer time, they will use you all well,
In winter you'd best stay at home with your girl.

CHORUS:
That's the rule of the railway makers,
Rare, good, jolly bankers, O.

On Monday morning, it's one of our rules
For every man to choose out his tools;
And they that come first do pick out the best,
And they that come after must just take the rest.

Now when that we come to the bottom run,
We fill our barrows right up to our chin,
We fill up our barrows, right up, breast high;
And if you can't wheel it, another will try.

And when that we come to the main plank wheel,
We lower our hands and stick fast on our heels;
For if the plank does bend or go,
Our ganger on top cries, 'Look out below'.

Our master he comes with his staff in his hand;
He knows very well how to measure the land.
He measures our dumpling, so deep and so wide,
He measures it well for his own side.

Now when we are struck by the frost or the snow,
We'll blow up our mess, boys, and off we will go;
We'll call to our time-keeper, without any damp,
To give us our time before we go on tramp.

On Saturday night we receive our pay;
It's then to the ale-house we go straightway.
And each sits his sweetheart upon his knee,
And we treat them well with the barley brew.

Last Saturday night, I received my full pay;
On Monday morning, I ran away.
I buzzed up the tommy shop and stopped the score,
And swore that I'd never go that road no more.

But when several months are gone and past,
Those pretty young girls got thick in the waist.
They run to buy cradles, they learn lullabies,
And wish that they still had their dear banker boys.

ANON.   27

A NEW SONG ON THE OPENING OF THE
BIRMINGHAM AND LIVERPOOL RAILWAY

On the fourth day of July, I recollect well,
What bustle there was in the morning I'll tell,
With the lads and young lasses so buxom and gay,
Delighted and talking about the railway.

CHORUS:
You may travel by steam, or so the folks say,
All the world over upon the railway.

To view the railroad, away they did go,
It's a great undertaking, you very well know;
It surpasses all others, believe me, it's true:
There's tunnels for miles that you have to go through.

There's coaches and carts to accommodate all,
The lame and the lazy, the great and the small;
If you wish for to ride, to be sure, you must pay,
To see all the fun, sir, upon the railway.

Colliers from Hampton and Bilston likewise
And Wedgebury nailers are struck with surprise;
To see the railroad, to be sure, they must go,
Dressed up in their best, they all cut a fine show.

The cobbler left all the old shoes in the shop;
Old women on crutches were seen for to hop;
And the tailor his customers would not obey,
But rode on his goose for to see the railway.

There was fat Dumpling Bet with young Jack the
     Moonraker,
There was buxom young Kit with the butcher
     and baker,
And Black Sal from Walsall with two wooden legs,
To see the railroad how she trudged on her pegs.

In London, I've heard said, there is a machine,
Invented for making young children by steam:
Such dear little creatures, full thirty a day,
For young engineers to supply the railway.

Come all you young fellows and let us be free,
Again fill the glasses, now merry we'll be;
Success to all trades in the reign of our queen,
And the boiling hot water that travels by steam.

ANON.

JOHNNY GREEN'S TRIP FRO' OWDHUM TO SEE THE MANCHESTER RAILWAY

Last New year's day eawr Nan hoo sed
Why Joan we'n bin near three yer wed
An sin the day to church I're led,
Theaw ne'er wur th'chap to treat one,
Awhoam this day aw will not stay
Awl ha me play – so aw moot say,
Theawst see th'Railway this very day,
So bless thee dunna fret mon.

Aw took an sowd me seawkin pig
For ready brass to Billy Brigg,
An looast me jacket just to rig
Me'sel in decent fettle,
Eawr Nan buck'd up ith best hoo cud,
An off we peg'd thro' Hollinwood
O'er Newton Yeoth past *Robin Hood*
An stopt at *Crown an Kettle*.

We seed sich lots o' Jerry shops,
Boh we'd na stay to drink ther slops,
Eendway we went and made to steps,
An just in toime we nick'd um,
For helter skelter, sich a crew
Wur cummin in fro Liverpoo'

Awm sure they cud no faster goo
If the devil in hell had kick'd um,

Aw shouted eawt an whirl'd me hat,
An whizz they coom at sich a bat,
Aw run so hard an puff'd an swat,
Boh aw cud naw keep with waggins,
When thinjun stopt an seet um deawn
Aw wundert wher they aw wur beawn,
They rode in callivans 'oth teawn,
Aw think to get ther baggins,

They coom awm sure at Leeds aw guess,
Two hundred mile it's eawr or less,
Neaw Ben, theaw loughs an winks at Bess
Becose theaw thinks awm loyink,
Theaw seed th'balloons fro Sawford goo,
Theaw seed foke run deawn Tinkers broo,
Boh it bangs um aw an th'races too –
Ecod it's next to floyink.

We seed tat coach wot Wellington
An awth greyt foke on day coom on,
They'll show it thee or any mon,

An tell thee aw ist axes.
Eawr Nan sed they'd ha sarv'd him reet,
To drag'd him on thro dry an weet,
An ridd'n him on both day an neet,
If he'd naw ta'en off the taxes

Boath Nan an me to roide had meeont,
Boh th'brass yo seen wur welly spent
So straightway up Knotmill we went,
An at th' sign oth Railway bated.
We cum by th'*Star* in Deansgate too,
An th'coachman theor look'd woeful blue,
Awm sure ther jaws han had nowt to doo,
Sin th'Liverpool Railway gated

We stopt to see that noice clock case
Leet up wi gas ith Firmary place,
A chap coom staring in my face,
An puff'd me een up fairly
Says Nan theawd best naw doot agen,
Aw gript me fist an look thee Ben.
If awd boh had me clogs just then,
Awd purr'd his ribs O rarely,

We coom straight whoam geet choilt to bed,
Aw fetch'd some beer fro th'owd *Nag's Yed*,
While Nan reach'd eawt some beef an bread

An bravely we mow'd away mon,
Its rare proime ale an drinks loike rum,
One pint a that's worth two of some
Aw had naw quite three quarts by gum
Boh me yed warch'd aw next day mon.

Aw yerd me uncle Nathan say,
They're gooink to make a new Railway,
Fro Manchester to Owdham – eh.
Aw wish it wur boh gated.
For weavers then to th'warehouse soon,
May tey ther cuts by twelve at noon,
An then theaw knows theyn save their shoon,
An not be awlus bated.

Theres weary wark ith papers – some
Say th' revolutions beawn to come,
An very loike to morn, by gum
Fo th'news is come by th' mail road
Theyn feeor eawr Nan to deeoth these chaps,
Hoo says – eh Joan awl wesh me caps,
Do thee tey down thee looms an traps
An we'n cut eawr stick bith Railroad.

Aw awlus sed yo known it too,
No mon cud tell what steam ud doo,
An if toth Owdfield lone yo'll goo

Yo'll find awm none mistaken.
Aw ne'er struck stroke this blessed day,
Aw know naw that eawr Nan'd say
Its dinner toime an if aw stay
Hool ate awth beoons an bacon.

NAVVY ON THE LINE

I am a navvy bold, that's tramped the country round, sir,
To get a job of work, where any can be found, sir.
I left my native home, my friends and my relations,
To ramble up and down and work in various stations.

CHORUS:
I'm a navvy, don't you see, I'm a navvy in my prime;
I'm a nipper, I'm a tipper, and I'm working on the line.

I left my native home on the first day of September,
That memorable day I still do remember.
I bundled up my kit, Sunday smock and cap put on, sir,
And wherever I do go, folks call me happy Jack, sir.

I've got a job of work in the lovely town of Bury,
And working on the line is a thing that makes me merry.
I can use my pick and spade, likewise my old
    wheelbarrow;
I can court the lasses, too, but don't intend to marry.

I worked a fortnight there, and then it come to pay-day,
And when I got my wages, I thought I'd have a play-day.
And then a little spree in High Street went quite handy,
Then I sat me down in Jenkinson's beside a Fanny
    Brandy.

I called for a pint of beer, and bid the old wench drink,
    sir,
But whilst she was a-drinking, she too at me did wink,
    sir.
Well, then we had some talk; in the back we had a rally;
Then jumped o'er brush and steel, and agreed we'd
    both live tally.

They called for liquors freely, the jug went quickly
    round, sir
That being my wedding day, I spent full many a crown,
    sir.
And when my brass was done, old Fanny went
    a-cadging,
And to finish up my spree, I went and sloped my
    lodgings.

Oh now I'm going to leave the lovely town of Bury;
I'm sorry for to leave you chaps, for I always found you
    merry.
So call for liquors freely, and drink away my dandy,
Here's a health to happy Jack, likewise to Fanny Brandy.

RUGBY TO PETERBOROUGH LINE
A Song from Bradshaw

By *Rockingham* and *Harborough* the road ran fair and
    wide,
And who would want a better way, to tramp it or to
    ride?
At *Wansford*, heads were shaken then, at *Wakerley* and
    Barrowden,
When first they saw the railwaymen invade the
    countryside.

The turf that fringed the King's highway was broad
    and fresh and green,
And if the road was deep in mud the grass was always
    clean.
– 'Twas horrid, at the railway's birth, from *Nassington*
    to *Theddingworth,*
To see the banks of naked earth the metals ran between!

At *Welford*, for the coaching horn, they heard the
    whistling steam,
The couplings clanked in *Castor*, for the clatter of the
    team;
And peasants walking in the dark near *Yelvertoft* and
    Stanford Park,
Would pause upon their way to mark the passing
    engine's gleam.

But now the grass has grown again upon the broken
    ground,
The whistling of the engines is an old, accustomed
    sound;
And down the line, from *Clifton Mill* as far as
    Orton Waterville,
Are little country stations still, where quiet can be
    found.

TIMETABLE

Kettering, Geddington
Corby and Weldon
Gretton, Harringworth
Manton for Uppingham

Oakham, Ashwell
Whissendine, Saxby
Melton Mowbray
Grimston, Dalby

Upper Broughton
Widmerpool, Plumtree
Edwalton, Nottingham
Change for Derby

(Sometimes poetry writes itself. This is virtually verbatim from a 1938 Bradshaw's Railway Guide.)

ENGINEERING

THE IRON STEED

In our black stable by the sea,
Five and twenty stalls you see –
Five and twenty strong are we:
The lanterns tossed the shadows round,
Live coals were scattered on the ground,
The swarthy ostlers echoing stept,
But silent all night long we slept.
Inactive we, the steeds of the day,
The shakers of the mountains, lay.
Earth's oldest veins our dam and sire,
Iron chimeras fed with fire.
All we, the unweary, lay at rest;
The sleepless lamp burned on our crest;
And in the darkness far and nigh,
We heard our iron compeers cry...

KING STEAM

Hurrah for the rail! for the stout iron rail,
　　A boon to both country and town,
From the very first day that the permanent way
　　And the far-famed fish-point was laid down.
'Tis destined, you'll find, to befriend all mankind,
　　To strew blessings all over the world;
Man's science, they say, gave it birth one fine day,
　　And the flag of King Steam was unfurled.

CHORUS:
Then hurrah for King Steam, whose wild whistle and scream
　　Gives notice to friends and to foes,
　　As he makes the dust fly, and goes thundering by,
So stand clear, and make room for King Steam.

Aye! a monarch, I say, hath he been from the day
　　He was born; on that glad happy hour,
Until now, when we know the vast debt that we owe
　　To his daring, his speed, and his power!
See the birds left behind, as he outstrips the wind
　　By the aid of key, sleeper and metal.
Great Watt little thought what a giant he'd caught,
　　When the infant was boiling a kettle.

They may tell, if they will, that our monarch can kill,
    'Tis a fact, I admit, and well know,
But fairly inquire, and there's this to admire,
    The fault is but rarely his own.
With the high and the low he's his failings, we know,
    And his moments of weakness, no doubt.
Since the world first began there were spots on the sun,
    Then why should King Steam be without?
      Then hurrah (etc.)

ROMANCE

'Romance!' the season-tickets mourn,
'*He* never ran to catch his train,
'But passed with coach and guard and horn –
'And left the local – late again!'
Confound Romance! . . . And all unseen
Romance brought up the nine-fifteen.

His hand was on the lever laid,
His oil-can soothed the worrying cranks,
His whistle waked the snowbound grade,
His fog-horn cut the reeking Banks;
By dock and deep and mine and mill
The Boy-god reckless laboured still!

Robed, crowned and throned, He wove his spell,
Where heart-blood beat or hearth-smoke curled,
With unconsidered miracle,
Hedged in a backward-gazing world:
Then taught His chosen bard to say:
'Our King was with us – yesterday!'

TO A GREAT WESTERN BROADGAUGE
ENGINE AND ITS STOKER

So! I shall never see you more,
You mighty lord of railway-roar;
The splendid stroke of driving-wheel,
The burnished brass, the shining steel,
Triumphant pride of him who drives
From Paddington to far St. Ives.
Another year, and then your place
Knows you no more; a pigmy race
Usurps the glory of the road,
And trails along a lesser load.
Drive on then, engine, drive amain,
Wrap me, like love, yet once again
A follower in your fiery train.

Drive on! and driving, let me know
The golden West, its warmth, its glow.
Pass Thames with all his winding maze,
Sweet Clifton dreaming in a haze;
And, farther yet, pass Taunton Vale,
And Dawlish rocks, and Teignmouth sail,
And Totnes, where the dancing Dart
Comes seaward with a gladsome heart;
Then let me feel the wind blow free
From levels of the Cornish sea.

Drive on! Let all your fiery soul,
Your puissant heart that scorns control,
Your burnished limbs of circling steel,
The throb, the pulse of driving-wheel,
O'erflood the breast of him whose gaze
Is set to watch your perilous ways,
Burn brighter in those eyes of vair,
Blow back the curly, close-cropped hair.
Ah! Western lad, would I might be
A partner in that ecstasy.

THE TAY BRIDGE DISASTER

Beautiful Railway Bridge of the Silv'ry Tay!
Alas! I am very sorry to say
That ninety lives have been taken away,
On the last Sabbath day of 1879
Which will be remember'd for a very long time.

When the train left Edinburgh
The passengers' hearts were light and felt no sorrow,
But Boreas blew a terrific gale,
Which made their hearts for to quail,
And many of the passengers with fear did say –
'I hope God will send us safe across the Bridge of Tay.'

So the train mov'd slowly along the Bridge of Tay,
Until it was about midway,
Then the central girders with a crash gave way,
And down went the train and passengers into the Tay!
The Storm Fiend did loudly bray,
Because ninety lives had been taken away,
On the last Sabbath day of 1879,
Which will be remember'd for a very long time.

It must have been an awful sight,
To witness in the dusky moonlight,
While the Storm Fiend did laugh, and angry did bray,

Along the Railway Bridge of the Silv'ry Tay.
I must now conclude my lay
By telling the world fearlessly without the least dismay,
That your central girders would not have given away,
At least many sensible men do say,
Had they been supported on each side with buttresses,
At least many sensible men confesses,
For the stronger we our houses do build,
The less chance we have of being killed.

CASEY JONES

Come *all* you rounders, if you wanta – *hear*
Story a*bout* a brave – *in*gineer.
Now, 'K. C.' – *Jones* – was this rounder's – *name*,
On a six-eight-wheeler, boys, he won – his – fame.
Caller called K.C. at a half-past – *four*,
Kissed his wife – at the station – *door*,
Mounted to the cabin with his orders in his hand,
Took his fare – well – trip – to the Promised – Land.

   Casey – Jones! – Mounted to the cabin –
   Casey – Jones! – with his orders in his hand –
   Casey – Jones! – Mounted to the cabin –
   Took his farewell – trip, to the Promised – Land.

'Put *in* yo' water, an' a-shovel in yo' *coal*,
Stick yo' head *out* the winda, watch them drivers – *roll*,
I'll *run* her – *till* she *leaves* the rail,
'Cause I'm eight hours *late* with that western – mail.'
Looked *at* his *watch*, an' his watch was – *slow*;
Looked *at* the water, an' the *water* was low.
Turned to the fireman, an' then he – *said*,
'We're gonna reach – Frisco, but we'll all – be – dead.'

   Casey – Jones! – Gonna reach – Frisco –
   Casey – Jones! – but we'll all – be dead –

Casey – Jones! – Gonna reach – Frisco –
Gonna reach – Frisco, but we'll all – be – dead.

K.C. pulled *up* – that Reno – *hill*,
Whistled for the crossin' with an *aw* – ful shrill –
Switchman *knew* – by the ingine's *moans* –
That the man *at* the throttle *was* K. C. *Jones.*
Pulled up – within – two *miles* of the place –
Number *Four* – starin' him – right in the face!
Turned to the fireman, says, 'Boy, better *jump*,
'Cause the's *two* locomotives that's a-gointa – *bump!*'

Casey – Jones! – Two – locomotives –
Casey – Jones! – that's a-gointa bump –
Casey – Jones! – Two – locomotives –
Two – Locomotives that's a-gointa – bump.

K.C. *said* – jes' befo' he – *died*,
'*Two – mo'* – roads, that I wanted to ride.'
Fireman – says – 'What *can* they – be?'
'It's the Southern – Pa*ci*fic, an' the Santa – *Fe*.'
Missis *Jones* sat *on* – her *bed*, a-sighin',
Jes' received a message that K.C. was dyin',
Says, '*Go* ta bed, chillun, an' *hush* yo' cryin',
'Cause you got another poppa on the Salt – Lake – Line.'

Missis Casey – Jones! – Got another poppa –
Missis Casey – Jones! – on the Salt – Lake – Line –
Missis Casey – Jones! – Got another poppa –
Got another poppa on the Salt – Lake – Line.

THE LITTLE RED CABOOSE
BEHIND THE TRAIN

Conductor he's a fine old man, his hair is turning grey,
  He works on in the sunshine and the rain.
And the angels all are sober, as he rides all alone,
  In that little red caboose behind the train.
'Twas many a year ago, his hair was black as jet,
  It's whiter now, his heart has known such pain
And I'll tell you all a story, a story that is true,
  Of that little red caboose behind the train.

He met her in September, she was so fair and sweet.
  Oftimes together they'd walk lovers' lane.
Never was a girl more fair, no sweeter ever rode
  In that little red caboose behind the train.
'Twas on a frosty morn, the cold north wind did blow.
  The cold had frozen up the window pane.
They were riding to the city, it was on their honeymoon,
  In that little red caboose behind the train.

The engineer had ridden that line for many years.
  He said the cold was driving him insane.
But he held on to that throttle, his pal was in the rear,
  In that little red caboose behind the train.
The fast express came roaring at ninety miles an hour.
  The brakie tried to see, but it was in vain,

For his fingers all were frozen. He said a silent prayer
   For that little red caboose behind the train.

'Twas after that collision, among the wreckage there,
   They found her body crushed amid blood stain.
Many were the tears and heartaches, and many were
     the prayers,
   For that little red caboose behind the train.
They laid her in the graveyard beside the railroad track.
   He still works in the sunshine and the rain.
And the angels all are sober, as he rides all alone
   In that little red caboose behind the train.

ANON.   55

TRAGIC INCIDENT

The trains are stopp'd, the MIGHTY CHIEFS OF FLAME
To quench their thirst the crystal water claim;
While from their post the great in crowds alight,
When, by a line-train, in its hasty flight,
Through striving to avoid it, Huskisson
By unforeseen mischance was over-run.
That stroke, alas! was death in shortest time;
Thus fell the great financier in his prime!
This fatal chance not only caused delay,
But damped the joy that erst had crown'd the day ...

At length the Steam-Chiefs with replenish'd force
To Manchester pursued their pageant course;
A grand reception there secure they found;
And though acclaim still made the air resound,
The blithe response was clogg'd with grief's alloy,
The fate of Huskisson still chill'd their joy.
The mutual greetings and the banquet o'er,
The Steam-Chiefs, in procession as before,
With equal pomp and eight-fold gorgeous train,

Forthwith returned to Liverpool again:
While still the eager crowds, we scarce need say,
Their progress hail'd with plaudits all the way.
Now in conclusion, 'twould be vain to tell,

How high at Liverpool was rapture's swell!
How rich the banquet and how choice the wines,
Where thus in state the mighty Arthur dines!
While eloquence, like the occasion, rare,
May be inferr'd, since Peel and Brougham were there!

T. BAKER

CYCLOPEAN

This circled cosmos whereof man is god
　　Has suns and stars of green and gold and red,
And cloudlands of great smoke, that range o'er range
　　Far floating, hide its iron heavens o'erhead.

God! Shall we ever honour what we are,
　　And see one moment ere the age expire,
The vision of man shouting and erect,
　　Whirled by the shrieking steeds of flood and fire?

Or must Fate act the same grey farce again,
　　And wait, till one, amid Time's wrecks and scars,
Speaks to a ruin here, 'What poet-race
　　Shot such cyclopean arches at the stars?'

THE EXPRESS

After the first powerful plain manifesto
The black statement of pistons, without more fuss
But gliding like a queen, she leaves the station.
Without bowing and with restrained unconcern
She passes the houses which humbly crowd outside,
The gasworks, and at last the heavy page
Of death, printed by gravestones in the cemetery.
Beyond the town there lies the open country
Where, gathering speed, she acquires mystery,
The luminous self-possession of ships on ocean.
It is now she begins to sing – at first quite low
Then loud, and at last with a jazzy madness –
The song of her whistle screaming at curves,
Of deafening tunnels, brakes, innumerable bolts.
And always light, aerial, underneath,
Retreats the elate metre of her wheels.
Steaming through metal landscape on her lines,
She plunges new eras of white happiness,
Where speed throws up strange shapes, broad curves
And parallels clean like the steel of guns.
At last, further than Edinburgh or Rome,
Beyond the crest of the world, she reaches night
Where only a low streamline brightness
Of phosphorus on the tossing hills is white.

Ah, like a comet through flame she moves entranced
Wrapt in her music no bird song, no, nor bough
Breaking with honey buds, shall ever equal.

ARE YE RIGHT THERE, MICHAEL?

Ye may talk of Columbus's sailing
Across the Atlantic sea
But he never tried to go railing
From Ennis as far as Kilkee.
You run for the train in the mornin'
The excursion train starting at eight,
You're there when the clock gives the warnin',
And there for an hour you will wait
And as you're waiting in the train
You'll hear the guard sing this refrain;

'Are ye right there, Michael? are ye right?
Do ye think that ye'll be there before the night?
Oh, ye've been so long in startin';
That ye couldn't say for sartin';
Still ye might now, Michael, so ye might!'

They find out where the engine's been hiding,
And it drags you to sweet Corofin;
Says the guard, 'Back her down on the siding,
There's the goods from Kilrush comin' in.'
Perhaps it comes in in two hours,
Perhaps it breaks down on the way;
'If it does,' says the guard, 'be the powers,
We're here for the rest of the day!'

And while you sit and curse your luck,
The train backs down into a truck!

'Are ye right there, Michael? are ye right?
Have ye got the parcel there for Missus White?
Oh, ye haven't! Oh, begorra!
Say it's comin' down tomorra
And it might now, Michael, so it might!'

At Lahinch the sea shines like a jewel,
With joy you are ready to shout,
When the stoker cries out,
'There's no fuel,
And the fire is taytotallay out.
But hand up that bit of a log there
I'll soon have ye out of the fix;
There's a fine clamp of turf in the bog there;'
And the rest go a-gatherin' sticks.
And while you're breaking bits off trees,
You hear some wise remarks like these:

'Are ye right there, Michael, are ye right?
Do ye think that ye can get the fire to light?
Oh, an hour you'll require,
For the turf it might be dryer,
Well it might now, Michael, so it might.'

Kilkee! Oh, you never get near it!
You're in luck if the train brings you back,
For the permanent way is so queer, it
Spends most of its time off the track.
Uphill the ould engin' is climbin'
While the passengers push with a will;
You're in luck when you reach Ennistymon,
For all the way home is downhill.
And as you're wobbling through the dark,
You hear the guard make this remark:

'Are ye right there, Michael? are ye right?
Do ye think that ye'll be home before it's light?
'Tis all dependin' whether
The ould engin' howlds together
And it might now, Michael, so it might!'

PERCY FRENCH

WAITING

'IF ALL THE TRAINS AT CLAPHAM JCTN'

If all the trains at Clapham Jctn
Were suddenly to cease to fctn
The people waiting in the stn
Would never reach their destintn.

ANON.

ON THE DEPARTURE PLATFORM

We kissed at the barrier; and passing through
She left me, and moment by moment got
Smaller and smaller, until to my view
     She was but a spot;

A wee white spot of muslin fluff
That down the diminishing platform bore
Through hustling crowds of gentle and rough
     To the carriage door.

Under the lamplight's fitful glowers,
Behind dark groups from far and near,
Whose interests were apart from ours,
     She would disappear,

Then show again, till I ceased to see
That flexible form, that nebulous white;
And she who was more than my life to me
     Had vanished quite....

We have penned new plans since that fair fond day,
And in season she will appear again –
Perhaps in the same soft white array –
     But never as then!

– 'And why, young man, must eternally fly
A joy you'll repeat, if you love her well?'
– O friend, nought happens twice thus; why,
     I cannot tell!

THE SEND-OFF

Down the close darkening lanes they sang their way
To the siding-shed,
And lined the train with faces grimly gay.

Their breasts were stuck all white with wreath and spray
As men's are, dead.

Dull porters watched them, and a casual tramp
Stood staring hard,
Sorry to miss them from the upland camp.

Then, unmoved, signals nodded, and a lamp
Winked to the guard.

So secretly, like wrongs hushed-up, they went.
They were not ours:
We never heard to which front these were sent;

Nor there if they yet mock what women meant
Who gave them flowers.

Shall they return to beating of great bells
In wild train-loads?
A few, a few, too few for drums and yells,

May creep back, silent, to village wells,
Up half-known roads.

DISTANT VIEW OF A PROVINCIAL TOWN

Besides those spires so spick and span
    Against an unencumbered sky
The old Great Western Railway ran
    When someone different was I.

St. Aidan's with the prickly nobs
    And iron spikes and coloured tiles –
Where Auntie Maud devoutly bobs
    In those enriched vermilion aisles:

St. George's where the mattins bell
    But rarely drowned the trains for prayer –
No Popish sight or sound or smell
    Disturbed that gas-invaded air:

St. Mary's where the Rector preached
    In such a jolly friendly way
On cricket, football, things that reached
    The simple life of every day:

And that United Benefice
    With entrance permanently locked, –
How Gothic, grey and sad it is
    Since Mr. Grogley was unfrocked!

The old Great Western Railway shakes
  The old Great Western Railway spins –
The old Great Western Railway makes
  Me very sorry for my sins.

IN A WAITING ROOM

On a morning sick as the day of doom
    With the drizzling grey
    Of an English May,
There were few in the railway waiting-room.
About its walls were framed and varnished
Pictures of liners, fly-blown, tarnished.
The table bore a Testament
For travellers' reading, if suchwise bent.

    I read it on and on,
And, thronging the Gospel of Saint John,
Were figures – additions, multiplications –
By some one scrawled, with sundry emendations;
    Not scoffingly designed,
    But with an absent mind, –
    Plainly a bagman's counts of cost,
    What he had profited, what lost;
And whilst I wondered if there could have been
    Any particle of a soul
    In that poor man at all,
    To cypher rates of wage
    Upon that printed page,
    There joined in the charmless scene
And stood over me and the scribbled book

      (To lend the hour's mean hue
      A smear of tragedy too)
A soldier and wife, with haggard look
Subdued to stone by strong endeavour;
      And then I heard
      From a casual word
They were parting as they believed for ever.
      But next there came
      Like the eastern flame
Of some high altar, children – a pair –
Who laughed at the fly-blown pictures there.
'Here are the lovely ships that we,
Mother, are by and by going to see!
When we get there it's 'most sure to be fine,
And the band will play, and the sun will shine!'

It rained on the skylight with a din
As we waited and still no train came in;
But the words of the child in the squalid room
Had spread a glory through the gloom.

DEPARTURE PLATFORM

Always to look like this
At the unmeeting place:
Scrambling of crowds and air
When the gilt clock-hands move
Across the wet moon-face
(Seen, cheek touching lip,
Through your distracting hair)
To enter time again
Where disappointments live
In shabby comradeship.

All this is nothing new

Still on the stroke of four
A wilderness of rail
Into which we have come
Feeling like all the lost
Ten tribes of Israel,
Maybe to see and hear
The hobbled tree of steam
Lofting between the wheels
Its paradisal hiss
Under a dripping roof;

The rain still falling now

To share a jealous dream
Of pert and slithering heels
In the rain's puddled glass,
Who have the time I leave,
And all the afternoon
A bitter nail, a clove,
A high, blind window pane
When the black pistons drive
Where but away from love.

Now there is nothing new

PERSHORE STATION, OR A LIVERISH JOURNEY FIRST CLASS

The train at Pershore station was waiting that Sunday
    night
Gas light on the platform, in my carriage electric light,
Gas light on frosty evergreens, electric on Empire
    wood,
The Victorian world and the present in a moment's
    neighbourhood.
There was no one about but a conscript who was
    saying good-bye to his love
On the windy weedy platform with the sprinkled stars
    above
When sudden the waiting stillness shook with the
    ancient spells
Of an older world than all our worlds in the sound of
    the Pershore bells.
They were ringing them down for Evensong in the
    lighted abbey near,
Sounds which had poured through apple boughs for
    seven centuries here.
With Guilt, Remorse, Eternity the void within me fills
And I thought of her left behind me in the
    Herefordshire hills.
I remembered her defencelessness as I made my heart
    a stone

Till she wove her self-protection round and left me on
my own.
And plunged in a deep self pity I dreamed of another
wife
And lusted for freckled faces and lived a separate life.
One word would have made her love me, one word
would have made her turn
But the word I never murmured and now I am left
to burn.
Evesham, Oxford and London. The carriage is new
and smart.
I am cushioned and soft and heated with a deadweight
in my heart.

AT THE RAILWAY STATION, UPWAY

'There is not much that I can do,
 For I've no money that's quite my own!'
 Spoke up the pitying child –
A little boy with a violin
At the station before the train came in, –
'But I can play my fiddle to you,
And a nice one 'tis, and good in tone!'

 The man in the handcuffs smiled;
The constable looked, and he smiled, too,
 As the fiddle began to twang;
And the man in the handcuffs suddenly sang
 With grimful glee:
 'This life so free
 Is the thing for me!'
And the constable smiled, and said no word,
As if unconscious of what he heard;
And so they went on till the train came in –
The convict, and boy with the violin.

THOMAS HARDY 79

RAILWAY NOTE

The station roofs curve off and line is lost
In white thick vapour. A smooth marble sun
Hangs there. It is the sun. An ermine frost
Edges each thorn and willow skeleton
Beyond the ghosts of goods-yard engines. Who
On earth will get the big expresses through?
But these men do.
We ride incredulous at the use and eyes
That pierce this blankness: like a sword-fish flies
The train with other trains ahead, behind,
Signalled with detonation, whistle, shout;
At the great junction stops.
Ticket-collectors board us and fling out
Their pleasantry as though
They liked things so,
Answering the talkative considerate kind,
'Not so bad now, but it's *been* bad you know.'

COUNTRY STATION

First she made a little garden
of sorrel stalks wedged among
some yellowy-brown moss-cushions

and fenced it with ice-lolly sticks
(there were just enough); then she
set out biscuit-crumbs on a brick

for the ants; now she sits on a
deserted luggage-trolley
to watch them come for their dinner.

It's nice here – cloudy but quite warm.
Five trains have swooshed through, and one
stopped, but at the other platform.

Later, when no one is looking,
she may climb the roof of that
low shed. Her mother is making

another telephone call (she
isn't crying any more).
Perhaps they will stay here all day.

FLEUR ADCOCK   81

'THERE WAS AN OLD MAN
AT A JUNCTION'

There was an Old Man at a Junction,
Whose feelings were wrung with compunction,
When they said 'The Train's gone!' He exclaimed
    'How forlorn!'
But remained on the rails of the Junction.

MORNING EXPRESS

Along the wind-swept platform, pinched and white,
The travellers stand in pools of wintry light,
Offering themselves to morn's long, slanting arrows,
The train's due; porters trundle laden barrows.
The train steams in, volleying resplendent clouds
    Of sun-blown vapour. Hither and about,
Scared people hurry, storming the doors in crowds.
    The officials seem to waken with a shout,
Resolved to hoist and plunder; some to the vans
Leap; others rumble the milk in gleaming cans.
Boys, indolent-eyed, from baskets leaning back,
    Question each face; a man with a hammer steals
Stooping from coach to coach; with clang and clack
    Touches and tests, and listens to the wheels.
Guard sounds a warning whistle, points to the clock
With brandished flag, and on his folded flock
Claps the last door: the monster grunts: 'Enough!'
Tightening his load of links with pant and puff.
Under the arch, then forth into blue day,
Glide the processional windows on their way,
And glimpse the stately folk who sit at ease
To view the world like kings taking the seas
In prosperous weather: drifting banners tell
    Their progress to the counties; with them goes
    The clamour of their journeying; while those
Who sped them stand to wave a last farewell.

SIEGFRIED SASSOON   83

THE RAILWAY JUNCTION

From here through tunnelled gloom the track
Forks into two; and one of these
Wheels onward into darkening hills,
And one toward distant seas.

How still it is; the signal light
At set of sun shines palely green;
A thrush sings; other sound there's none,
Nor traveller to be seen –

Where late there was a throng. And now,
In peace awhile, I sit alone;
Though soon, at the appointed hour,
I shall myself be gone.

But not their way: the bow-legged groom,
The parson in black, the widow and son,
The sailor with his cage, the gaunt
Gamekeeper with his gun,

That fair one, too, discreetly veiled –
All, who so mutely came, and went,
Will reach those far nocturnal hills,
Or shores, ere night is spent.

I nothing know why thus we met –
Their thoughts, their longings, hopes, their fate:
And what shall I remember, except –
The evening growing late –

That here through tunnelled gloom the track
Forks into two; of these
One into darkening hills leads on,
And one toward distant seas?

AT EUSTON STATION

Yon is the train I used to take
  In the good days of yore
When I went home for love's dear sake,
  I who go home no more.

The station lights flare in the wind,
  The night is blurred with rain,
And there was someone, old and kind,
  Who will not come again.

Oh, that's an Irish voice I hear,
  And that's an Irish face,
And these will come when dawn is near
  To the belovèd place.

And these will see when day is grey
  And lightest winds are still
The long coast-line by Dublin Bay
  With exquisite hill on hill.

I would not follow if I might,
  Who came so oft of old;
No window-pane holds me a light,
  The warm hearth-fire is cold.

There is the train I used to take.
  Be blest from shore to shore,
O land of love and of heart-break!
  But I go home no more.

THE WAYSIDE STATION

Here at the wayside station, as many a morning,
I watch the smoke torn from the fumy engine
Crawling across the field in serpent sorrow.
Flat in the east, held down by stolid clouds,
The struggling day is born and shines already
On its warm hearth far off. Yet something here
Glimmers along the ground to show the seagulls
White on the furrows' black unturning waves.

But now the light has broadened.
I watch the farmstead on the little hill,
That seems to mutter: 'Here is day again'
Unwillingly. Now the sad cattle wake
In every byre and stall,
The ploughboy stirs in the loft, the farmer groans
And feels the day like a familiar ache
Deep in his body, though the house is dark.
The lovers part
Now in the bedroom where the pillows gleam
Great and mysterious as deep hills of snow,
An inaccessible land. The wood stands waiting
While the bright snare slips coil by coil around it,
Dark silver on every branch. The lonely stream
That rode through darkness leaps the gap of light,
Its voice grown loud, and starts its winding journey
Through the day and time and war and history.

SKIMBLESHANKS: THE RAILWAY CAT

There's a whisper down the line at 11.39
When the Night Mail's ready to depart,
Saying 'Skimble where is Skimble has he gone to hunt
    the thimble?
We must find him or the train can't start.'
All the guards and all the porters and the
    stationmaster's daughters
They are searching high and low,
Saying, 'Skimble where is Skimble for unless he's
    very nimble
Then the Night Mail just can't go.'
At 11.42 then the signal's nearly due
And the passengers are frantic to a man –
Then Skimble will appear and he'll saunter to the rear:
He's been busy in the luggage van!
        He gives one flash of his glass-green eyes
           And the signal goes 'All clear!'
        And we're off at last for the northern part
           Of the Northern hemisphere!

You may say that by and large it is Skimble who's
    in charge
Of the Sleeping Car Express.
From the driver and the guards to the bagmen
    playing cards

He will supervise them all, more or less.
Down the corridor he paces and examines all
  the faces
Of the travellers in the First and in the Third;
He establishes control by a regular patrol
And he'd know at once if anything occurred.
He will watch you without winking and he sees what
  you are thinking
And it's certain that he doesn't approve
Of hilarity and riot, so the folk are very quiet
When Skimble is about and on the move.
   You can play no pranks with Skimbleshanks!
    He's a cat that cannot be ignored;
   So nothing goes wrong on the Northern Mail
    When Skimbleshanks is aboard.

Oh! it's very pleasant when you have found your
  little den
With your name written up on the door.
And the berth is very neat with a newly folded sheet
And there's not a speck of dust on the floor.
There is every sort of light – you can make it dark
  or bright;
There's a handle that you turn to make a breeze.
There's a funny little basin you're supposed to wash
  your face in
And a crank to shut the window if you sneeze.

Then the guard looks in politely and will ask you
        very brightly
'Do you like your morning tea weak or strong?'
But Skimble's just behind him and was ready to
        remind him,
For Skimble won't let anything go wrong.
        And when you creep into your cosy berth
            And pull up the counterpane,
        You ought to reflect that it's very nice
        To know that you won't be bothered by mice –
        You can leave all that to the Railway Cat,
            The Cat of the Railway Train!

In the watches of the night he is always fresh
        and bright;
Every now and then he has a cup of tea
With perhaps a drop of Scotch while he's keeping on
        the watch,
Only stopping here and there to catch a flea.
You were fast asleep at Crewe and so you never knew
That he was walking up and down the station;
You were sleeping all the while he was busy at
        Carlisle,
Where he greets the stationmaster with elation.
But you saw him at Dumfries, where he speaks to
        the police
If there's anything they ought to know about:

When you get to Gallowgate there you do not have
     to wait –
For Skimbleshanks will help you to get out!
        He gives you a wave of his long brown tail
           Which says: 'I'll see you again!
        You'll meet without fail on the Midnight Mail
           The Cat of the Railway Train.'

DILTON MARSH HALT

Was it worth keeping the Halt open,
    We thought as we looked at the sky
Red through the spread of the cedar-tree,
    With the evening train gone by?

Yes, we said, for in summer the anglers use it,
    Two and sometimes three
Will bring their catches of rods and poles and perches
    To Westbury, home to tea.

There isn't a porter. The platform is made of sleepers.
    The guard of the last up-train puts out the light
And high over lorries and cattle the Halt unwinking
    Waits through the Wiltshire night.

O housewife safe in the comprehensive churning
    Of the Warminster launderette!
O husband down at the depot with car in car-park!
    The Halt is waiting yet.

And when all the horrible roads are finally done for,
    And there's no more petrol left in the world to burn,
Here to the Halt from Salisbury and from Bristol
    Steam trains will return.

'THERE WAS AN OLD MAN
AT A STATION'

There was an Old Man at a Station,
Who made a promiscuous oration;
But they said, 'Take some snuff! – You have talk'd
    quite enough
You afflicting old man at a Station!'

THE TRAIN

The train will come tomorrow year,
The signals clamber into signs,
The gates will open on the track
Where weeds have grown among the lines.

A murmur in the listening air
Besides the heart's emphatic beat
Will rise beyond the junction bridge
Out of the summer's static heat,

And round the distant, anxious bend
Engine and carriages appear.
But on a sultry afternoon
Your waiting hope could turn to fear.

Confronted with achieved desires
You may see nothing more to do
Than shrink from noise and turn away
As every devil thunders through.

ALAN BROWNJOHN

CHANGING AT YORK

A directory that runs from B to V,
the Yellow Pages' entries for HOTELS
and TAXIS torn out, the smell of dossers' pee,
saliva in the mouthpiece, whisky smells –
I remember, now I have to phone,
squashing a *Daily Mail* half full of chips,
to tell the son I left at home alone
my train's delayed, and get cut off by the pips,
how, phoning his mother, late, a little pissed,
changing at York, from some place where I'd read,
I used 2p to lie about the train I'd missed
and ten more to talk my way into some girl's bed
and, in this same kiosk with the stale, sour breath
of queueing callers, drunk, cajoling, lying,
consoling his grampa for his granny's death,
how I heard him, for the first time ever, crying.

TRAVELLING

(⅟₄₅) SOUTHERN RAILWAY. (707)

FROM WATERLOO TO

AMESBURY

ADLEWHAT? 1

Adlestrop? I don't remember the name.
When high speed trains make unscheduled halts
It's such a bore. They spend millions of pounds
And still can't stop them developing faults.

FROM A RAILWAY CARRIAGE

Faster than fairies, faster than witches,
Bridges and houses, hedges and ditches;
And charging along like troops in a battle,
All through the meadows the horses and cattle:
All of the sights of the hill and the plain
Fly as thick as driving rain;
And ever again, in the wink of an eye,
Painted stations whistle by.

Here is a child who clambers and scrambles,
All by himself and gathering brambles;
Here is a tramp who stands and gazes,
And there is the green for stringing the daisies!
Here is a cart run away in the road
Lumping along with man and load;
And here is a mill, and there is a river:
Each a glimpse and gone for ever!

'THERE WAS A YOUNG LADY OF SWEDEN'

There was a Young Lady of Sweden,
Who went by the slow train to Weedon;
When they cried, 'Weedon Station!' she made no
    observation,
But she thought she should go back to Sweden.

FAINTHEART IN A RAILWAY TRAIN

At nine in the morning there passed a church,
At ten there passed me by the sea,
At twelve a town of smoke and smirch,
At two a forest of oak and birch,
    And then, on a platform, she:

A radiant stranger, who saw not me.
I said, 'Get out to her do I dare?'
But I kept my seat in my search for a plea,
And the wheels moved on. O could it but be
    That I had alighted there!

THE EVERLASTING PERCY

I used to be a fearful lad,
The things I did were downright bad;
And worst of all were what I done
From seventeen to twenty-one
On all the railways far and wide
From sinfulness and shameful pride.

For several years I was so wicked
I used to go without a ticket,
And travelled underneath the seat
Down in the dust of people's feet,
Or else I sat as bold as brass
And told them 'Season', in first-class.
In 1921, at Harwich,
I smoked in a non-smoking carriage;
I never knew what Life nor Art meant,
I wrote 'Reserved' on my compartment,
And once (I was a guilty man)
I swopped the labels in guard's van.

From 1922 to 4.
I leant against the carriage door
Without a-looking at the latch;
And once, a-leaving Colney Hatch,
I put a huge and heavy parcel

Which I were taking to Newcastle,
Entirely filled with lumps of lead,
Up on the rack above my head;
And when it tumbled down, oh Lord!
I pulled communication cord.

The guard came round and said, 'You mule!
What have you done, you dirty fool?'
I simply sat and smiled, and said
'Is this train right for Holyhead?'
He said 'You blinking blasted swine,
You'll have to pay the five-pound fine.'
I gave a false name and address,
Puffed up with my vaingloriousness.

At Bickershaw and Strood and Staines
I've often got on moving trains,
And once alit at Norwood West
Before my coach had come to rest.
A window and a lamp I broke
At Chipping Sodbury and Stoke
And worse I did at Wissendine:
I threw out bottles on the line
And other articles as be
Likely to cause grave injury
To persons working on the line –
That's what I did at Wissendine.

I grew so careless what I'd do
Throwing things out, and dangerous too,
That, last and worst of all I'd done,
I threw a great sultana bun
Out of the train at Pontypridd –
It hit a platelayer, it did,
I thought that I should have to swing
And never hear the sweet birds sing.
The jury recommended mercy,
And that's how grace was given to Percy.

ADLESTROP

Yes. I remember Adlestrop –
The name, because one afternoon
Of heat the express-train drew up there
Unwontedly. It was late June.

The steam hissed. Someone cleared his throat.
No one left and no one came
On the bare platform. What I saw
Was Adlestrop – only the name

And willows, willow-herb, and grass,
And meadowsweet, and haycocks dry,
No whit less still and lonely fair
Than the high cloudlets in the sky.

And for that minute a blackbird sang
Close by, and round him, mistier,
Farther and farther, all the birds
Of Oxfordshire and Gloucestershire.

DAWN

Opposite me two Germans snore and sweat.
   Through sullen swirling gloom we jolt and roar.
We have been here for ever: even yet
   A dim watch tells two hours, two aeons, more.
The windows are tight-shut and slimy-wet
   With a night's foetor. There are two hours more;
Two hours to dawn and Milan; two hours yet.
   Opposite me two Germans sweat and snore....

One of them wakes, and spits, and sleeps again.
The darkness shivers. A wan light through the rain
Strikes on our faces, drawn and white. Somewhere
A new day sprawls; and, inside, the foul air
Is chill, and damp, and fouler than before....
Opposite me two Germans sweat and snore.

FROM THE GREAT WESTERN

These small West Country towns where year by year
Newly elected mayors oppose reforms
Their last year's Worships promised – down the roads
Large detached houses, Croydons of the West,
Blister in summer heat; striped awnings hang
Over front doors, and those geraniums,
Retired tradesmen love to cultivate,
Blaze in the gravel. From more furtive streets
Unmarried mothers leave for London. Girls
Who had such promise suddenly lose their looks.
Small businesses go bankrupt. Corners once
Familiar for a shuttered toll gate house
Are smoothed away to make amenities.
The copper beech, the bunchy sycamore
And churchyard limes are felled. Among their stumps
The almond tree shall flourish. Corn Exchange –
On with the Poultry Show! and Cemet'ry,
With your twin chapels, safely gather in
Church and dissent from small West Country towns
Where year by year,
Newly elected Mayors oppose reforms.

LOOSE COUPLING 1
LOOSE COUPLING OR INTER-CITY INTERCOURSE
(calling at all stations from Paddington to Oxford, via Maidenhead Junction)

A lisping blond on Paddington
Showed girls his royal oak,
One left the train at Westbourne Park,
Would not act on his joke.

RESTAURANT CAR

Fondling only to throttle the nuzzling moment
Smuggled under the table, hungry or not
We roughride over the sleepers, finger the menu,
Avoid our neighbours' eyes and wonder what

Mad country moves beyond the steamed-up window
So fast into the past we could not keep
Our feet on it one instant. Soup or grapefruit?
We had better eat to pass the time, then sleep

To pass the time. The water in the carafe
Shakes its hips, both glass and soup-plate spill,
The tomtom beats in the skull, the waiters totter
Along their invisible tightrope. For good or ill,

For fish or meat, with single tickets only
Our journey still in the nature of a surprise,
Could we, before we stop where all must change,
Take one first look and catch our neighbours' eyes?

EXPRESS

As the through-train of words with white-hot whistle
Shrills past the heart's mean halts, the mind's full stops,
With all the signals down; past the small town
Contentment, and the citizens all leaning
And loitering parenthetically
In waiting-rooms, or interrogative on platforms;
Its screaming mouth crammed tight with urgent
    meaning,
– I, by it borne on, look out and wonder
To what happy or calamitous terminus.
I am bound, what anonymity or what renown.
O if at length into Age, the last of all stations,
It slides and slows, and its smoky mane of thunder
Thins out, and I detrain; when I stand in that place
On whose piers and wharves, from all sources and seas,
Men wearily arrive I pray that still
I may have with me my pities and indignations.

ADLEWHAT? 2

It was hot, you say? I've no idea –
Rolling-stock's air-conditioned these days,
And the weather always seems threatening
Through tinted glass and double glaze.

THE WHITSUN WEDDINGS

That Whitsun, I was late getting away:
    Not till about
One-twenty on the sunlit Saturday
Did my three-quarters-empty train pull out,
All windows down, all cushions hot, all sense
Of being in a hurry gone. We ran
Behind the backs of houses, crossed a street
Of blinding windscreens, smelt the fish-dock; thence
The river's level drifting breadth began,
Where sky and Lincolnshire and water meet.

All afternoon, through the tall heat that slept
    For miles inland,
A slow and stopping curve southwards we kept.
Wide farms went by, short-shadowed cattle, and
Canals with floatings of industrial froth;
A hothouse flashed uniquely: hedges dipped
And rose: and now and then a smell of grass
Displaced the reek of buttoned carriage-cloth
Until the next town, new and nondescript,
Approached with acres of dismantled cars.

At first, I didn't notice what a noise
    The weddings made
Each station that we stopped at: sun destroys

The interest of what's happening in the shade,
And down the long cool platforms whoops and skirls
I took for porters larking with the mails,
And went on reading. Once we started, though,
We passed them, grinning and pomaded, girls
In parodies of fashion, heels and veils,
All posed irresolutely, watching us go,

As if out on the end of an event
    Waving goodbye
To something that survived it. Struck, I leant
More promptly out next time, more curiously,
And saw it all again in different terms:
The fathers with broad belts under their suits
And seamy foreheads; mothers loud and fat;
An uncle shouting smut; and then the perms,
The nylon gloves and jewellery-substitutes,
The lemons, mauves, and olive-ochres that

Marked off the girls unreally from the rest.
    Yes, from cafés
And banquet-halls up yards, and bunting-dressed
Coach-party annexes, the wedding-days
Were coming to an end. All down the line
Fresh couples climbed aboard: the rest stood round;
The last confetti and advice were thrown,
And, as we moved, each face seemed to define

Just what it saw departing: children frowned
At something dull; fathers had never known

Success so huge and wholly farcical;
    The women shared
The secret like a happy funeral;
While girls, gripping their handbags tighter, stared
At a religious wounding. Free at last,
And loaded with the sum of all they saw,
We hurried towards London, shuffling gouts of steam.
Now fields were building-plots, and poplars cast
Long shadows over major roads, and for
Some fifty minutes, that in time would seem

Just long enough to settle hats and say
    I nearly died,
A dozen marriages got under way.
They watched the landscape, sitting side by side
– An Odeon went past, a cooling tower,
And someone running up to bowl – and none
Thought of the others they would never meet
Or how their lives would all contain this hour.
I thought of London spread out in the sun,
Its postal districts packed like squares of wheat:

There we were aimed. And as we raced across
    Bright knots of rail

Past standing Pullmans, walls of blackened moss
Came close, and it was nearly done, this frail
Travelling coincidence; and what it held
Stood ready to be loosed with all the power
That being changed can give. We slowed again,
And as the tightened brakes took hold, there swelled
A sense of falling, like an arrow-shower
Sent out of sight, somewhere becoming rain.

GREAT CENTRAL RAILWAY
SHEFFIELD VICTORIA TO BANBURY

'Unmitigated England'
   Came swinging down the line
That day the February sun
   Did crisp and crystal shine.
Dark red at Kirkby Bentinck stood
   A steeply gabled farm
'Mid ash trees and a sycamore
   In charismatic calm.
A village street – a manor house –
   A church – then, tally ho!
We pounded through a housing scheme
   With tellymasts a-row,
Where cars of parked executives
   Did regimented wait
Beside administrative blocks
   Within the factory gate.
She waved to us from Hucknall South
   As we hooted round a bend,
From a curtained front-room window did
   The diesel driver's friend.
Through cuttings deep to Nottingham
   Precariously we wound;
The swallowing tunnel made the train
   Seem London's Underground.

Above the fields of Leicestershire
   On arches we were borne
And the rumble of the railway drowned
   The thunder of the Quorn;
And silver shone the steeples out
   Above the barren boughs;
Colts in a paddock ran from us
   But not the solid cows;
And quite where Rugby Central is
   Does only Rugby know.
We watched the empty platform wait
   And sadly saw it go.
By now the sun of afternoon
   Showed ridge and furrow shadows
And shallow unfamiliar lakes
   Stood shivering in the meadows.
Is Woodford church or Hinton church
   The one I ought to see?
Or were they both too much restored
   In 1883?
I do not know. Towards the west
   A trail of glory runs
And we leave the old Great Central line
   For Banbury and buns.

THE SINGING CAT

It was a little captive cat
   Upon a crowded train
His mistress takes him from his box
   To ease his fretful pain.

She holds him tight upon her knee
   The graceful animal
And all the people look at him
   He is so beautiful.

But oh he pricks and oh he prods
   And turns upon her knee
Then lifteth up his innocent voice
   In plaintive melody.

He lifteth up his innocent voice
   He lifteth up, he singeth
And to each human countenance
   A smile of grace he bringeth.

He lifteth up his innocent paw
   Upon her breast he clingeth
And everybody cries, Behold
   The cat, the cat that singeth.

He lifteth up his innocent voice
    He lifteth up, he singeth
And all the people warm themselves
    In the love his beauty bringeth.

LOOSE COUPLING 4

Alone in his compartment, he
Was straightening his dress,
When 'Will you sleep with me?' inquired
A winsome Scottish lass.

'I LIKE TO SEE IT LAP
THE MILES –'

I like to see it lap the Miles –
And lick the Valleys up –
And stop to feed itself at Tanks –
And then – prodigious step

Around a Pile of Mountains –
And supercilious peer
In Shanties – by the sides of Roads –
And then a Quarry pare

To fit its Ribs
And crawl between
Complaining all the while
In horrid – hooting stanza –
Then chase itself down Hill –

And neigh like Boanerges –
Then – punctual as a Star
Stop – docile and omnipotent

THE SLEEPING PASSENGER

The train relinquishes the station,
The doors slap shut, the posters slide,
And the windows move, in green gradation,
On to opening fans of countryside
Whose revolutions intrude no shape
Into your sleep's untroubled void.

Your father begot you in his sleep
– And your mother was probably sleeping too.
You have never wakened up,
Even when your eyes open blue
Windows of astonishment
Into a world they do not know,
They see it as an awkward instant
– A something not to be inquired into.

Though all should founder – or at least shake,
You ripen like fruit on a sunny wall,
Too cosy asleep ever to wake:
Waiting to be picked, or to fall.
Your untroubled blood dictates
Growth asleep, like a vegetable.

You are unacquainted with the fates,
For you there is no precipice

Between this state and other states.
What was, what will be, and what is
Indistinguishably harden
Into the rails whose rhythm marries
Your dream to its mechanical burden.

You do not talk of the atom bomb,
The weather, or what grows in your garden.
Unbothered by daily news or doom
You have taken conscience and let it slip
Back to the limbo where it came from.
Others may be puzzled, you can cope,
You are master of your situation
Because you have never sized it up.
You have already reached your destination.

A MIND'S JOURNEY TO DISS

Dear Mary,
   Yes, it will be bliss
To go with you by train to Diss,
Your walking shoes upon your feet;
We'll meet, my sweet, at Liverpool Street.
That levellers we may be reckoned
Perhaps we'd better travel second;
Or, lest reporters on us burst,
Perhaps we'd better travel first.
Above the chimney-pots we'll go
Through Stepney, Stratford-atte-Bow
And out to where the Essex marsh
Is filled with houses new and harsh
Till, Witham pass'd, the landscape yields
On left and right to widening fields,
Flint church-towers sparkling in the light,
Black beams and weather-boarding white,
Cricket-bat willows silvery green
And elmy hills with brooks between,
Maltings and saltings stack and quay
And, somewhere near, the grey North Sea;
Then further gentle undulations
With lonelier and less frequent stations,
Till in the dimmest place of all

The train slows down into a crawl
And stops in silence.... Where is this?
Dear Mary Wilson, this is Diss.

ADLEWHAT? 3

Haycocks and meadowsweet? I wouldn't know.
I never looked outside the train,
Just drank canned beer from a plastic cup
Until the damned thing started again.

'LIKE THE TRAIN'S BEAT'

Like the train's beat
Swift language flutters the lips
Of the Polish airgirl in the corner seat.
The swinging and narrowing sun
Lights her eyelashes, shapes
Her sharp vivacity of bone.
Hair, wild and controlled, runs back:
And gestures like these English oaks
Flash past the windows of her foreign talk.

The train runs on through wilderness
Of cities. Still the hammered miles
Diversify behind her face.
And all humanity of interest
Before her angled beauty falls,
As whorling notes are pressed
In a bird's throat, issuing meaningless
Through written skies; a voice
Watering a stony place.

From SUMMONED BY BELLS
*(John Betjeman's childhood home moves from Highgate
to Chelsea)*

I missed the trains, the few North London trains,
The frequent Underground to Kentish Town.
Here in a district only served by bus,
Here on an urban level by the Thames –
I never really liked the Chelsea house.
'It's simply sweet, Bess,' visitors exclaimed,
Depositing their wraps and settling down
To a nice rubber. 'So artistic, too.'
To me the house was poky, dark and cramped,
Haunted by quarrels and the ground-floor ghost.
I'd slam behind me our green garden door –
Well do I recollect that bounding thrill! –
And hare to Cheyne Gardens – free! free! free! –
By Lawrence Street and Upper Cheyne Row,
Safe to the tall red house of Ronnie Wright.

    Great was my joy with London at my feet –
All London mine, five shillings in my hand
And not expected back till after tea!
Great was our joy, Ronald Hughes Wright's and mine,
To travel by the Underground all day
Between the rush hours, so that very soon
There was no station, north to Finsbury Park,
To Barking eastwards, Clapham Common south,

No temporary platform in the west
Among the Actons and the Ealings, where
We had not once alighted. Metroland
Beckoned us out to lanes in beechy Bucks –
Goldschmidt and Howland (in a wooden hut
Beside the station): 'Most attractive sites
Ripe for development'; Charrington's for coal;
And not far off the neo-Tudor shops.
We knew the different railways by their smells.
The City and South reeked like a changing-room;
Its orange engines and old rolling-stock,
Its narrow platforms, undulating tracks,
Seemed even then historic. Next in age,
The Central London, with its cut-glass shades
On draughty stations, had an ozone smell –
Not seaweed-scented ozone from the sea
But something chemical from Birmingham.
When, in a pause between the stations, quiet
Descended on the carriage we would talk
Loud gibberish in angry argument,
Pretending to be foreign.

ADLEWHAT? 4

A blackbird sang? Look, where've you been?
Modern coaches are sound-proof, see;
All I could hear was the guard on the tannoy
Somewhere in Area Thirty-Three.

From SUMMONED BY BELLS

Come, Hygiene, goddess of the growing boy,
I here salute thee in Sanatogen!
Anaemic girls need Virol, but for me
Be Scott's Emulsion, rusks, and Mellin's Food,
Cod-liver oil and malt, and for my neck
Wright's Coal Tar Soap, Euthymol for my teeth.
Come, friends of Hygiene, Electricity
And those young twins, Free Thought and clean
    Fresh Air:
Attend the long express from Waterloo
That takes us down to Cornwall. Tea-time shows
The small fields waiting, every blackthorn hedge
Straining inland before the south-west gale.
The emptying train, wind in the ventilators,
Puffs out of Egloskerry to Tresméer
Through minty meadows, under bearded trees
And hills upon whose sides the clinging farms
Hold Bible Christians. Can it really be
That this same carriage came from Waterloo?
On Wadebridge station what a breath of sea
Scented the Camel valley! Cornish air,
Soft Cornish rains, and silence after steam...
As out of Derry's stable came the brake

To drag us up those long, familiar hills,
Past haunted woods and oil-lit farms and on
To far Trebetherick by the sounding sea.

HOME-COMING TO CORNWALL

A landslide on the line, the train diverted
Back up the valley of the red Exe in spate
Rich with Devonshire soil, flooding the green
Meadows, swirling round the wooded bends,
The December quality of light on boles of trees,
Black and shining out of the gathering dark,
The sepia brushwork against the western skies
Filtering the last watercolour light.
(Why should the eyes fill with tears, as if
One should not look upon the like again?
So many eyes have seen that coign of wood,
That curve of river, the pencil screen of trees.)
I fall asleep; the train feels slowly round
The unfamiliar northern edge of Dartmoor.
It is night and we are entering Cornwall strangely:
The sense of excitement wakens me, to see
Launceston perched on a shoulder like Liège,
The young moon white above the moving clouds.
The train halts in the valley where monks prayed,
Under the castle-keep the Normans ruled
And Edward the Black Prince visited. We stop
At every wayside halt, a signal-box,
An open waiting shed, a shrub or two,
A friendly voice out of the night, a lamp –
Egloskerry, Tresmeer and Otterham –
And out upon the shaven moonlit moor.

A LOCAL TRAIN OF THOUGHT

Alone, in silence, at a certain time of night,
Listening, and looking up from what I'm trying to
    write,
I hear a local train along the Valley. And 'There
Goes the one-fifty', think I to myself; aware
That somehow its habitual travelling comforts me,
Making my world seem safer, homelier, sure to be
The same tomorrow; and the same, one hopes, next year.
'There's peacetime in that train.' One hears it disappear
With needless warning whistle and rail-resounding
    wheels.
'That train's quite like an old familiar friend', one feels.

INCIDENT IN AUGUST

When the Circle train was held up by a signal
    Between Gloucester Road and High Street (Ken)
In the battering dog-day heat of August
    We sweated and mopped our brows. And then
We saw in the cutting, amid the loosestrife
    And butterflies looping though bindweed trails,
A boy who lay drinking, straight from the bottle,
    When, of course, he was paid to look after the rails.

High stood the sun and the heat-haze shimmered,
    The crickets shrilled to the burnished tracks;
But our minds and the motors throbbed together,
    Insisting 'You're late. You mustn't relax,
You mustn't look backward, you mustn't look ...
      Southward?'
(Oh, the linemen stood by in the hills of Var
And leaned on their spades as the trains went
      past them
    And swigged red wine from a great stone jar.)

Now, the boy in the sunlight was drinking water –
    Or beer at the best. It might have been Beaune
Or Chateauneuf, but a London embankment.
    Was not the slopes of the Côtes-du-Rhône.
Still, a Mistral blew out of dry Vaucluse,

A Mistral blew over South-West Ten...
Till the train pulled out from Mondragon-sur-Lez
  As the points changed back towards High Street
    (Ken).

NIGHT MAIL
(Commentary for a G.P.O. Film)

I

This is the Night Mail crossing the Border,
Bringing the cheque and the postal order,

Letters for the rich, letters for the poor,
The shop at the corner, the girl next door.

Pulling up Beattock, a steady climb:
The gradient's against her, but she's on time.

Past cotton-grass and moorland boulder,
Shovelling white steam over her shoulder,

Snorting noisily, she passes
Silent miles of wind-bent grasses.

Birds turn their heads as she approaches,
Stare from bushes at her blank-faced coaches.

Sheep-dogs cannot turn her course;
They slumber on with paws across.

In the farm she passes no one wakes,
But a jug in a bedroom gently shakes.

II

Dawn freshens. Her climb is done.
Down towards Glasgow she descends,
Towards the steam tugs yelping down a glade of cranes,
Towards the fields of apparatus, the furnaces
Set on the dark plain like gigantic chessmen.
All Scotland waits for her:
In dark glens, beside pale-green lochs,
Men long for news.

III

Letters of thanks, letters from banks,
Letters of joy from girl and boy,
Receipted bills and invitations
To inspect new stock or to visit relations,
And applications for situations,
And timid lovers' declarations,
And gossip, gossip from all the nations,
News circumstantial, news financial,
Letters with holiday snaps to enlarge in,
Letters with faces scrawled on the margin,
Letters from uncles, cousins and aunts,
Letters to Scotland from the South of France,
Letters of condolence to Highlands and Lowlands,

Written on paper of every hue,
The pink, the violet, the white and the blue,
The chatty, the catty, the boring, the adoring,
The cold and official and the heart's outpouring,
Clever, stupid, short and long,
The typed and the printed and the spelt all wrong.

IV

Thousands are still asleep,
Dreaming of terrifying monsters
Or a friendly tea beside the band in Cranston's or
     Crawford's:
Asleep in working Glasgow, asleep in well-set
     Edinburgh,
Asleep in granite Aberdeen,
They continue their dreams,
But shall wake soon and hope for letters,
And none will hear the postman's knock
Without a quickening of the heart.
For who can bear to feel himself forgotten?

NOSTALGIA

You loved them too: those locos motley gay
That once seemed permanent as their own way? –
The Midland 'lake', the Caledonia blue;
The Brighton 'Stroudleys' in their umber hue;
North Western 'Jumbos', shimmeringly black,
That sped, shrill-whistled, on their 'Premier' track;
And all a forest's tints of green – G.C.,
G.N., G.W., L.T.S., H.B.,
South Western, Highland, 'Chatham': many more
Both on our own and on the Emerald shore?
Did you, beneath a sooty Oldham sky,
Think dour the 'Aspinalls' of L. and Y.,
Or, in the gloom of the Five Towns, admire
The cheerful, sturdy, red North Staffordshire?
Do you remember how the Suffolk sun
Gleamed on a blue Great Eastern 'Hamilton'?
In Wessex did you keep slow company
With the 'tanks' (royal) of the S. and D.,
That waited, as it seemed, for crack of doom
(While they performed strange rites) at Templecombe?
Across the Fens and Broadland did you reach,
And come – in course of time – to Cromer (Beach)
Behind a khaki M. and G.N.J.,
And was the 'pea soup' to your liking – say! –
Of the N.B. that took us over Forth

On our first wizard journey Further North?
The Johnson 'singles', Drummond 4–4–0s!
Were ever engines lovelier than those?
What treasured names they bore – *Sir Francis Drake,*
Swallow, Lysander, Lady of the Lake,
Courier, Gladstone, Glowworm, Lorna Doone,
Titan, Apollo, Jeanie Deans, Typhoon …
And in their wake what rainbow splendour ran:
The bronze-green coaches of the Cambrian;
G.N.S. red and white; North Eastern 'plum';
'Salmon' that struck one young observer dumb
At grim old Waterloo; the varnished teak
That, North or South, was never far to seek,
But had for apogee East Coast Joint Stock
That left King's Cross each morning, ten o'clock –
Though many held this did not equal quite
The West Coast purple-brown and (spilt-milk) white.

Those Furness trains – red, white, and blue – at Grange!
That 'orange' touch at Manchester (Exchange);
At Central the dark oak of Cheshire Lines?
Or – what the memory most of all enshrines:
The crown and consummation of our dreams! –
Those great 'joint' hubs where many colour-schemes
Converged to hold us under such a spell:
York, Cambridge, Perth, or Carlisle (Citadel)? …
The high 'bird-cages' of L.C. and D.?

Those dismal Broad Street arks one used to see
Above one ere (in hardly prouder state!)
One trundled up the bank at Bishopsgate? . . .
Those little Emett lines which 'also ran',
Saucily mocking at the march of man –
Festiniog, Southwold, Wantage, Isle of Wight,
Lynton and Barnstaple, East Suffolk Light? . . .
Yes, I remember! But I will not flog
My muse to furnish the whole catalogue.

'Each to his choice.' Although my youth was bred
Amid the comfortable Midland red,
And though for long, wherever I might roam,
M.R. to me spelled certitude and home,
Yet all my exiled Western blood took fire
When – a small boy, in snowy-starched attire –
I first changed trains at Bristol (Temple Meads).
Awhile my tastes were fickle; but the seeds
Sown there have proved the stubbornest by far:
Upon my heart is graved G.W.R.
And when I came to live near Brunel's wall,
Between the red cliffs and the rise and fall
Of Devon waves, I thought long years to see,
In ever-more-familiar livery,
The 'Dutchman' or the 'Limited' swing by,
Washed by the Channel spray.
                    Hope born to die!

MUSING

RAILWAY RHYMES

When books are pow'rless to beguile
And papers only stir my bile,
For solace and relief I flee
To *Bradshaw* or the *A B C.*
And find the best of recreations
In studying the names of stations.
There is not much among the *A*'s
To prompt enthusiastic praise,
But *B* is infinitely better,
And there are gems in ev'ry letter.
The only fault I have with Barnack
Is that it rhymes with DR. HARNACK;
Babon, Beluncle Halt, Bodorgan
Resound like chords upon the organ,
And there's a spirit blithe and merry
In Evercreech and Egloskerry.
Park Drain and Counter Drain, I'm sure,
Are hygienically pure,
But when æsthetically viewed
They seem to me a little crude.
I often long to visit Frant,
Hose, Little Kimble and Lelant:
And, if I had sufficient dollars,
Sibley's (for Chickney) and Neen Sollars;
Shustoke and Smeeth my soul arride,

And likewise Sholing, Sole Street, Shide,
But I'm afraid my speech might go
Awry on reaching Spooner Row.

In serious mood I often bend
My thoughts to Ponder and his End,
And when I'm feeling dull and down
The very name of Tibshelf Town
Rejoices me, while Par and Praze
And Pylle and Quy promote amaze.

Of all the Straths, a numerous host,
Strathbungo pleases me the most,
While I can court reluctant slumber
By murmuring thy name, Stogumber.
Were I beginning life anew
From Swadlincote I'd take my cue,
But shun as I would shun the scurvy
The perilous atmosphere of Turvey.
But though the tuneful name of Horbling
Incites to further doggerel warbling,
And Gallions, Goonbell, Gamlingay
Are each deserving of a lay,
No railway bard is worth his salt
Who cannot bear to call a 'Halt'.

LOOSE COUPLING 7

'How tactile her strong fingers are!
How sweet her pang-born cries!'
He mused, while goring with a will
On her train-shaken thighs.

RAILWAY SCRAPBOOK

Dockside stations
Estuary halts
Trolleys for luggage
Platelayers' huts
Steamy warm buffets
Station clock hands
Weighing machines
Post Office vans
Sidings and signals
Newspapers sweets
Cycles in cardboard
Platform seats
Coalyards and taxis
Pincers on tickets
Gaslight on blossom
Pigeons in baskets
Fire buckets red
Timetables white
Posters for seasides
Booking halls bright
Bridges and cuttings
Telephone wires
Tunnels and viaducts
Waiting room fires

MIDNIGHT ON THE GREAT WESTERN

In the third-class seat sat the journeying boy,
   And the roof-lamp's oily flame
Played down on his listless form and face,
Bewrapt past knowing to what he was going,
     Or whence he came.

In the band of his hat the journeying boy
   Had a ticket stuck; and a string
Around his neck bore the key of his box,
That twinkled gleams of the lamp's sad beams
     Like a living thing.

What past can be yours, O journeying boy
   Towards a world unknown,
Who calmly, as if incurious quite
On all at stake, can undertake
     This plunge alone?

Knows your soul a sphere, O journeying boy,
   Our rude realms far above,
Whence with spacious vision you mark and mete
This region of sin that you find you in,
     But are not of?

THOMAS HARDY

MONODY ON THE DEATH OF
ALDERSGATE STREET STATION

Snow falls in the buffet of Aldersgate station,
    Soot hangs in the tunnel in clouds of steam.
City of London! before the next desecration
    Let your steepled forest of churches be my theme.

Sunday Silence! with every street a dead street,
    Alley and courtyard empty and cobbled mews,
Till 'tingle tang' the bell of St. Mildred's Bread Street
    Summoned the sermon taster to high box pews,

And neighbouring towers and spirelets joined the
      ringing
    With answering echoes from heavy commercial walls
Till all were drowned as the sailing clouds went singing
    On the roaring flood of a twelve-voiced peal from
      Paul's.

Then would the years fall off and Thames run slowly;
    Out into marshy meadow-land flowed the Fleet:
And the walled-in City of London, smelly and holy,
    Had a tinkling mass house in every cavernous street.

The bells rang down and St. Michael Paternoster
　　Would take me into its darkness from College Hill,
Or Christ Church Newgate Street (with St. Leonard
　　　　Foster)
　　Would be late for Mattins and ringing insistent still.

Last of the east wall sculpture, a cherub gazes
　　On broken arches, rosebay, bracken and dock,
Where once I heard the roll of the Prayer Book phrases
　　And the sumptuous tick of the old west gallery clock.

Snow falls in the buffet of Aldersgate station,
　　Toiling and doomed from Moorgate Street puffs
　　　　the train,
For us of the steam and the gas-light, the lost
　　　　generation,
　　The new white cliffs of the City are built in vain.

THE MISSED TRAIN

How I was caught
Hieing home, after days of allure,
And forced to an inn – small, obscure –
At the junction, gloom-fraught.

How civil my face
To get them to chamber me there –
A roof I had scorned, scarce aware
That it stood at the place.

And how all the night
I had dreams of the unwitting cause
Of my lodgment. How lonely I was;
How consoled by her sprite!

Thus onetime to me ...
Dim wastes of dead years bar away
Then from now. But such happenings to-day
Fall to lovers, may be!

Years, years as shoaled seas,
Truly, stretch now between! Less and less
Shrink the visions then vast in me. – Yes,
Then in me: Now in these.

TWO WARS

Professing loud energy, out of the junction departed
The branch-line engine. The small train rounded
      the bend
Watched by us pilgrims of summer, and most by me, –
Who had known this picture since first my travelling
      started,
And knew it as sadly pleasant, the usual end
Of singing returns to beloved simplicity.

The small train went from view behind the plantation,
Monotonous, – but there's a grace in monotony!
I felt its journey, I watched in imagination
Its brown smoke spun with sunshine wandering free
Past the great weir with its round flood-mirror beneath,
And where the magpie rises from orchard shadows,
And among the oasts, and like a rosy wreath
Mimicking children's flower-play in the meadows.

The thing so easy, so daily, of so small stature
Gave me another picture: of war's warped face
Where still the sun and the leaf and the lark praised
      Nature,
But no little engine bustled from place to place;
When summer succeeded summer, yet only ghosts
Or to-morrow's ghosts could venture hand or foot

In the track between the terrible telegraph-posts, –
The end of all things lying between the hut
Which lurked this side, and the shattered local train
That.
    So easy it was; and should that come again –.

COMMUTERS

The slack faces
Of those in the train
Watch the bum-paper
In their sweaty hands.

Like folk in privies
They lean forward, each alone
Their visceral lives
Sagging within the skeleton.

If this is hope, they have it
The carriage will defecate
On the usual platform
They will find the amorous night.

THE METROPOLITAN RAILWAY
Baker Street station buffet

Early Electric! With what radiant hope
    Men formed this many-branched electrolier,
Twisted the flex around the iron rope
    And let the dazzling vacuum globes hang clear,
And then with hearts the rich contrivance fill'd
Of copper, beaten by the Bromsgrove Guild.

Early Electric! Sit you down and see,
    'Mid this fine woodwork and a smell of dinner,
A stained-glass windmill and a pot of tea,
    And sepia views of leafy lanes in PINNER, –
Then visualize, far down the shining lines,
Your parents' homestead set in murmuring pines.

Smoothly from HARROW, passing PRESTON ROAD,
    They saw the last green fields and misty sky,
At NEASDEN watched a workmen's train unload,
    And, with the morning villas sliding by,
They felt so sure on their electric trip
That Youth and Progress were in partnership.

And all that day in murky London Wall
    The thought of RUISLIP kept him warm inside;
At FARRINGDON that lunch hour at a stall

He bought a dozen plants of London Pride;
While she, in arc-lit Oxford Street adrift,
Soared through the sales by safe hydraulic lift.

Early Electric! Maybe even here
    They met that evening at six-fifteen
Beneath the hearts of this electrolier
    And caught the first non-stop to WILLESDEN GREEN,
Then out and on, through rural RAYNER'S LANE
To autumn-scented Middlesex again.

Cancer has killed him. Heart is killing her.
    The trees are down. An Odeon flashes fire
Where stood their villa by the murmuring fir
    When 'they would for their children's good conspire'.
Of their loves and hopes on hurrying feet
Thou art the worn memorial, Baker Street.

THE TOURIST'S ALPHABET

A is the affable guard whom you square:
B is the *Bradshaw* which leads you to swear:
C is the corner you fight to obtain:
D is the draught of which others complain:
E are the enemies made for the day:
F is the frown that you wear all the way:
G is the guilt that you feel going third:
H is the humbug by which you're deterred:
I is the insult you'll get down the line:
J is the junction where you'll try to dine:
K is the kettle of tea three weeks old:
L are the lemon drops better unsold:
M is the maiden who says there's no meat:
N is the nothing you thus get to eat:
O is the oath that you use – and do right:
P is the paper to which you *don't* write:
Q are the qualms to directors unknown:
Ř is the row which you'll find all your own:
S is the smash that is 'nobody's fault':
T is the truth, that will come to a halt:
U is the pointsman – who's up the whole night:
V is the verdict that says it's 'all right'.
W stands for wheels flying off curves:
X for express that half shatters your nerves:
Y for the yoke from your neck that you fling,
and Z for your zest as you cut the whole thing!

THE SPIRITUAL RAILWAY

In memory of
WILLIAM PICKERING
who died Decr 24. 1845 aged 30 years
also RICHARD EDGER
who died Decr 24. 1845 aged 24 years.

The Line to heaven by Christ was made
With heavenly truth the Rails are laid,
From Earth to Heaven the Line extends.
To Life Eternal where it ends

Repentance is the Station then
Where Passengers are taken in,
No Fee for them is there to pay
For Jesus is himself the way

God's Word is the first Engineer
It points the way to Heaven so dear,
Through tunnels dark and dreary here
It does the way to Glory steer.

God's Love the Fire, his Truth the Steam,
Which drives the Engine and the Train,
All you who would to Glory ride,
Must come to Christ, in him abide

In First and Second, and Third Class,
Repentance, Faith and Holiness,
You must the way to Glory gain
Or you with Christ will not remain

Come then poor Sinners, now's the time
At any Station on the Line.
If you'll repent and turn from sin
The Train will stop and take you in.

THE MAN IN THE BOWLER HAT

I am the unnoticed, the unnoticeable man:
The man who sat on your right in the morning train:
The man you looked through like a windowpane:
The man who was the colour of the carriage, the
    colour of the mounting
Morning pipe smoke.

I am the man too busy with a living to live,
Too hurried and worried to see and smell and touch:
The man who is patient too long and obeys too much
And wishes too softly and seldom.

I am the man they call the nation's backbone,
Who am boneless – playable catgut, pliable clay:
The Man they label Little lest one day
I dare to grow.

I am the rails on which the moment passes,
The megaphone for many words and voices:
I am graph, diagram,
Composite face.

I am the led, the easily-fed,
The tool, the not-quite-fool,
The would-be-safe-and-sound,

The uncomplaining bound,
The dust fine-ground,
Stone-for-a-statue waveworn pebble-round.

I REMEMBER, I REMEMBER

Coming up England by a different line
For once, early in the cold new year,
We stopped, and, watching men with number-plates
Sprint down the platform to familiar gates,
'Why, Coventry!' I exclaimed. 'I was born here.'

I leant far out, and squinnied for a sign
That this was still the town that had been 'mine'
So long, but found I wasn't even clear
Which side was which. From where those cycle-crates
Were standing, had we annually departed

For all those family hols? ... A whistle went:
Things moved. I sat back, staring at my boots.
'Was that,' my friend smiled, 'where you "have
        your roots"?'
No, only where my childhood was unspent,
I wanted to retort, just where I started:

By now I've got the whole place clearly charted.
Our garden, first: where I did not invent
Blinding theologies of flowers and fruits,
And wasn't spoken to by an old hat.
And here we have that splendid family

I never ran to when I got depressed,
The boys all biceps and the girls all chest,
Their comic Ford, their farm where I could be
'Really myself'. I'll show you, come to that,
The bracken where I never trembling sat,

Determined to go through with it; where she
Lay back, and 'all became a burning mist'.
And, in those offices, my doggerel
Was not set up in blunt ten-point, nor read
By a distinguished cousin of the mayor,

Who didn't call and tell my father *There
Before us, had we the gift to see ahead* –
'You look as if you wished the place in Hell,'
My friend said, 'judging from your face.' 'Oh well,
I suppose it's not the place's fault,' I said.

'Nothing, like something, happens anywhere.'

THOUGHTS IN A TRAIN

No doubt she is somebody's mistress,
    With that Greta Garbo hair,
As she sits, mascara-lidded,
    In the corner seat over there.

But why, if she's somebody's mistress,
    Is she travelling up in a third?
Her luggage is leather, not plastic,
    Her jewelry rich and absurd.

'Oh I am nobody's mistress:
    The jewels I wear, you see,
Were, like this leather luggage,
    A present from Mummy to me.

'If you want to get on with the Government,
    You've got to be like it, I've heard;
So I've booked my suite in the Ritz Hotel
    And I'm travelling up in a Third.'

THE BRANCH LINE

This poem relates to the closing of the line from
Sidmouth Junction to Exmouth in 1967.

One train was the last.
Decorated with a crowd
Of people who like last things,
Not normally travellers,
Mostly children and their fathers,
It left to a theatrical blast
As the guard for once played
At his job, with mixed feelings.

Photographers were there,
For the only time perhaps
Since the railway groped
Down into these shires
First of all, and the squires
Fretted about their deer.
There were flags and a few maps,
And cheers as the signal dropped.

The platform is now old
And empty, but still shows
The act of waiting.
Beyond it the meadows,

Where once the toy shadows
Of funnel and smoke bowled,
Are pure green, and no echoes
Squeeze into the cutting.

The villages that gave
The stations their names
Were always out of sight,
Behind a hill, up a lane,
Dead, except when a train
Fetched somebody forth alive.
But now no one at all comes
Out of them by this route.

The level-crossing gates
Guard passers-by from nothing
Now. The railway's bite
Is dislocated by time,
Too out-of-date to harm
Like a gummy old cat's.
The road is the frightening
Power, the current favourite....

PATRICIA BEER   169

THE RAILWAY CHILDREN

When we climbed the slopes of the cutting
We were eye-level with the white cups
Of the telegraph poles and the sizzling wires.

Like lovely freehand they curved for miles
East and miles west beyond us, sagging
Under their burden of swallows.

We were small and thought we knew nothing
Worth knowing. We thought words travelled the wires
In the shiny pouches of raindrops,

Each one seeded full with the light
Of the sky, the gleam of the lines, and ourselves
So infinitesimally scaled

We could stream through the eye of a needle.

THE METAPHOR NOW STANDING
AT PLATFORM 8

will separate at Birmingham New Street, and passengers
for the South West who sit for safety reasons in the rear
    carriages
will find themselves at Shit Creek Central without a
    paddle
or a valid ticket. No end of fancy talking will save them.

Parents and their children are today invited
to the engine of the metaphor, and may touch the dead
    man's handle.
Cow-catchers? Fried bacon on the footplateman's shovel?
    People,
please, this is 1990 not the Wild West.

You kids licking the tips of your pencils, I could talk
of the age of steam, riding the great Similitudes
into the record books. Take heart, a boy
could do worse than be a spotter of metaphors.

Here is the buffet car at the centre
of the metaphor, where hot buttered toast
and alcoholic beverages will certainly be mentioned.
In the next breath, lunch will be served.

171

This is not the allegorical boat train.
This is not the symbolic seaplane.
Madam, life is not a destination but a journey; sweet
that your friends should want to meet you there,
    but stupid.

Passengers, as part of our Transports of Delight
    programme
let me welcome this morning's poets. Beginning at the
    guard's van
they will troubadour the aisle reciting their short but
    engaging pieces.
Sir, I understand you have a reservation?

Feet off the seats, please. Lady, for the last time,
extinguish that cigarillo. This is a metaphor I'm
    running here
not a jamboree, and as soon as we get that straight
we're rolling. Till then, no one goes nowhere.

UNIVERSITY

On the settling of birds, this man blesses
                      his daughter.
She'll split fast for Paddington, then slide
                      east
which may as well be the black beyond
                      of Calcutta.

The low long curving train opening its
                      mouth
gulps from his hands her bags to a far-side
                      seat.
He gawps from his thin-rivered, working
                      town.

The train roars, the tracks beyond humped
                      with light.
The rucksack'd man with whom her eyes
                      meet...
Five birds pluck their wings off the train
                      and fly.

HARVISTON END

I looked out of the train,
    And I suddenly saw the empty station
    As we hurtled through, with a hollow roar...
'Harviston End'... It was dark and dead;
Thick dandelions choking the flower-bed,
Torn posters that flapped on the porter's shed,
    A broken window-pane,
      The waiting-room's shuttered desolation,
        The padlock on the booking-office door....

      Rrring...Rrring...Rrring...

I remember that platform bell,
    Which started the quiet station once an hour.
'Harviston End'...White pebbles used to spell
    The name along the borders, all in flower
With fierce geranium, lobelia and stocks;
    Sweet alyssum, and a golden privet hedge...
There was always a labelled bicycle, or a box
Of seedlings at the platform's edge
When a train was expected;
    Or a basket of pigeons in the shade,
Drawling and crooning, waiting to be collected...
    In the luggage office (where I was sometimes
      weighed

As a great treat, on the station scales)
    There was a musky smell of bran, and paraffin;
While, outside, sunlight dazzled upon the rails
    And on the bright advertisements (enamelled tin –
Three pen-nibs, and a splash of inky blue);
    And the air soft with tar, the summer smell...
And the chuff of a steam-train drowsing through
    The hazy hills...And the sound of the bell...

        Rrring...Rrring...Rrring...

And now the platform bell will ring no more.
    They will not come again,
        Those summers of youth and exultation;
New trains must run, and new tracks must wind,
And a place out of sight is soon out of mind –
And 'Harviston End' has been left behind...
    As we hurtled through, with a hollow roar,
        I looked out of the train,
            And I suddenly saw the empty station.

INDEX OF AUTHORS

ACKNOWLEDGMENTS

The editor would like to thank Philip Wilkinson for his suggestions and Elizabeth Raven-Hill for her invaluable help.

Thanks are due to the following copyright holders for permission to reprint:

FLEUR ADCOCK: 'Country Station' by Fleur Adcock from *Poems 1960–2000*, Bloodaxe Books, 2000. KENNETH ALLOTT: 'The Departure Platform' by Kenneth Allott. Reproduced with the kind permission of Professor Miriam Allott. SIMON ARMITAGE: 'The Metaphor Now Standing at Platform 8' by Simon Armitage, from *Kid* by Simon Armitage. Reprinted by permission of Faber & Faber Limited. W. H. AUDEN: 'Night Mail' by W. H. Auden. Reprinted by permission of Faber & Faber Limited. PATRICIA BEER: 'The Branch Line' by Patricia Beer, from *Collected Poems*. Reprinted by permission of Carcanet Press Limited. JOHN BETJEMAN: 'Distant View of a Provincial Town', 'The Metropolitan Railway', 'Monody on the Death of Aldersgate Street Station', 'Pershore Station, *or* a Liverish Journey First Class', 'From the Great Western', 'Great Central Railway Sheffield Victoria to Banbury', 'Dilton Marsh Halt', 'A Mind's Journey to Diss', 'Thoughts in a Train', two extracts from *Summoned by Bells* © John Betjeman by permission of the Estate of John Betjeman. PETER BLACK: 'The Man in the Bowler Hat' by Peter Black. Originally published in 1943. Found in *Poetry of the Forties* (page 233). EDMUND BLUNDEN: 'Two Wars' and 'Railway Note' by Edmund Blunden (Copyright © Estate of Mrs Claire Blunden 1940) are reproduced by permission of PFD (www.pfd.co.uk) on behalf of the Estate of Mrs Claire Blunden. ALAN BROWNJOHN: 'The Train' by Alan Brownjohn. Reprinted with permission from the poet. WALTER DE LA MARE: 'The Railway Junction' by Walter de la Mare from *The Complete Poems of Walter de la Mare* (1975 reprint). Reprinted with permission from The Literary Trustees of Walter de la Mare and The Society of Authors as their representative. T. S. ELIOT: 'Skimbleshanks: The Railway Cat' by T. S. Eliot. Reprinted by permission of Faber & Faber Limited. COLIN ELLIS: 'Rugby to Peterborough Line' © Colin Ellis. PERCY FRENCH: 'Are ye right there, Michael?' from *Percy French's Songbook*, Ossian Publications. C. L. GRAVES: 'Railway Rhymes' by C. L. Graves. Reproduced with permission of Punch Limited. www.punch.co.uk TONY HARRISON: 'Changing at York' by Tony Harrison, from *Tony Harrison: Collected Poems* & *Selected Poems* (Penguin, 2007 & 1987). Copyright © by Tony Harrison. Reproduced with kind permission from the author. SEAMUS HEANEY: 'The Railway Children' by Seamus Heaney. Reprinted by permission of Faber & Faber

Limited. E. V. KNOX: 'The Everlasting Percy' by E. V. Knox. Reproduced with permission of Punch Limited. www.punch.co.uk PHILIP LARKIN: 'The Whitsun Weddings' and 'Like the train's beat' by Philip Larkin. Reprinted by permission of Faber & Faber Limited. 'I Remember, I Remember' by Philip Larkin is reprinted from *The Less Deceived* by permission of The Marvell Press, England and Australia. PETER LING: 'Harviston End' by Peter Ling. Reproduced with permission of Punch Limited. www.punch.co.uk R. P. LISTER 'Nostalgia' by R. P. Lister. Reproduced with permission of Punch Limited. www.punch.co.uk LOUIS MACNEICE 'Restaurant Car' by Louis MacNeice from *Collected Poems*. Reprinted with permission from David Higham Associates. BRYAN MORGAN: 'Incident in August' by Bryan Morgan. Reproduced with permission of Punch Limited. www.punch.co.uk EDWIN MUIR: 'The Wayside Station' by Edwin Muir. Reprinted by permission of Faber & Faber Limited. DALJIT NAGRA: 'University' from *Look We Have Coming to Dover!* (Faber, 2007) by Daljit Nagra. Reprinted by permission of Faber & Faber Limited. 'MR PUNCH': 'The Tourist's Alphabet' from *Mr Punch's Railway Book*. Reproduced with permission of Punch Limited. www.punch.co.uk W. R. RODGERS: 'Express' by W. R. Rodgers from *Poems* (1993). Reprinted by kind permission of the Estate of W. R. Rodgers and The Gallery Press, Loughcrew, Oldcastle,

County Meath, Ireland. A. L. ROWSE: 'Homecoming to Cornwall' by A. L. Rowse. Reproduced with permission from Johnson & Alcock Limited. SIEGFRIED SASSOON: 'Morning Express' and 'A Local Train of Thought' by Siegfried Sassoon. Reproduced with permission from Ms Barbara Levy. C. H. SISSON: 'Commuters' by C. H. Sisson, from *In the Trojan Ditch*. Reprinted by permission of Carcanet Press Limited. STEVIE SMITH: 'The Singing Cat' by Stevie Smith. Reprinted by permission of the Estate of James MacGibbon. STEPHEN SPENDER: 'The Express' from *New Collected Poems* by Stephen Spender © 2004. Reprinted by kind permission of the Estate of Sir Stephen Spender. TIRESIAS (ROGER GREEN): 'Loose Coupling' 1, 4 and 7 and 'Adlewhat?' 1, 2, 3 and 4 from *Notes from Overground* by Tiresias (Roger Green), Paladin, 1984.

186